OPTIONS
TRADING
STRATEGIES

THE FIRST INVESTORS GUIDE TO KNOW THE
SECRETS OF OPTIONS TRADING STRATEGIES.
LEARN TRADING BASICS TO INCREASE YOUR
EARNINGS AND ACQUIRE THE BETTER
STRATEGIES

ANDREW ELDER

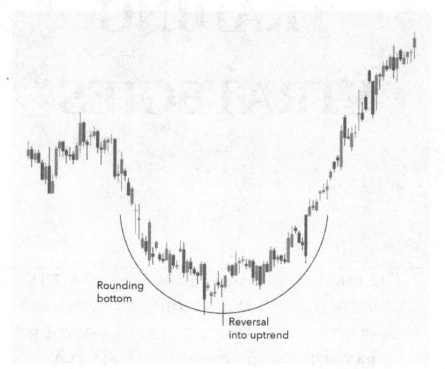

Rounding
bottom

Reversal
into uptrend

original author of this work can be in any fashion deemed liable for any hardship or damages that may befall them after undertaking the information described herein.

Additionally, the information in the following pages is intended only for informational purposes and should thus be thought of as universal. As befitting its nature, it is presented without assurance regarding its prolonged validity or interim quality. Trademarks that are mentioned are done without written consent and can in no way be considered an endorsement from the trademark holder.

TABLE OF CONTENT

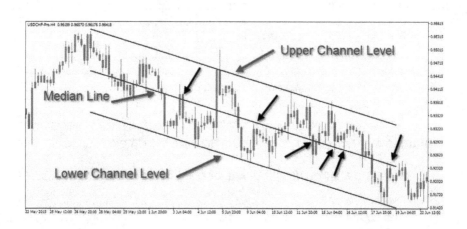

Introduction

Before you dive into day trading, it helps to know a little bit about what it is and isn't. This is not investing, which means you buy a stake in an asset that you hold onto hope it will build a profit over some time. The amount of time you hold on to it depends on you. Most of the time, an investor will hold it for many years, even decades. They also look at the type of business they are investing in. They investigate the companies to make sure they stay away from litigation, have good products, keep debts paid, and make good profits.

Day trading is the opposite of this. It means that you buy and sell stocks in one day. Day traders can use their own or borrowed money to invest in stocks and make profits off small price changes in highly liquid stocks. They still follow the wisdom of long-term investors: buy low, sell high. Day traders simply do this in a shorter amount of time.

A typical day for a trader will look a little like this. At 10 AM the trade chooses to buy 1,000 shares of a certain stock. When it starts to rise at 10:15, they sell the stock. If it had risen by half when they sold it, they made a $500 profit, minus commission. Assuming the trader uses Scottrade; commission could be anywhere from $7 to $27, which means their profit would be around \$493 to \$473. Then they also have to consider their taxes. When a stock has been held for less than a year, taxes will be based on your gain rate, and this may be as high as 35%. Investments are typically taxed no higher than 20%. This means tax planning should be an important part of your day.

If the profit looks small to you, remember, day traders make many trades throughout the day, often upwards of 25 to 30. This means profits are multiplied by high trade volume. To cut back on risks, they don't keep stocks overnight because a lot can change in that time. Announcements by the corporation and events can increase the market volatility, so a trader has to be available and can respond quickly. As opposed to long-term investors that will wait and think through things and look at information, day traders will act quickly and decide on things a few minutes or even seconds.

There are also some other types of trading options that lie between these extremes. You have swing trading, in which you hold onto stocks for a couple of days. There is position trading, which means you hold onto stocks for weeks or months. They all have their risks, and day trading tends to be the riskiest and most controversial.

History

The popularity of day trading is still fairly new. Different events and rulings over the past 100 years made day trading what it is. The following are the most important things that have happened in the day trading career that has made it so popular.

Traders used the first ticker tape in 1867, which meant it was easier for them to communicate information on transactions that took place on the exchange. Most brokers that traded on the Stock Exchange in New York kept close offices so they could get a regular tape feed.

At the height of one of the most popular bull markets, in 1928, traders couldn't access direct markets. This meant they had to use a broker to place an order from the information on ticker tapes.

The NASDAQ was created in 1971 by the NASD.

In 1975, the SEC came up with new rules which got rid of fixed commissions. This was the first time in more than 180 years that the market competition would set the trading fees. A lot of firms, including Charles Schwab, began giving clients discount rates for trades. This began the discount brokerage era.

In 1987, the majority of trades were done over the phone. This enabled the firms that bought and sold NASDAQ to avoid small investors that would try and call in trades during the crash in October. The SEC responded to this problem by creating the SOES, which is the small order entry system, which gave 1,000 shares or fewer priority.

At the dot-com craze height in 1997, people began to view technology stocks as a bull market. This was also a time where the internet started to become easier to use for everybody. Many of the current trading companies made their first websites. This helped small traders have access to price quotes and activities, which helped to provide everybody with a level playing field.

The attention today trading continued to grow in 1999. The SEC chairman, Arthur Levitt, testified to Congress that he had estimated the number of day traders was around 7,000.

He also said that the number of investors that used the internet was around 5 million. During this time, negative headlines about day trading began to circle.

One of the negative headlines was when Mark Barton shot up a day trading office in Atlanta. This made people think that day trading was way too stressful. Then two weeks later, the North American Securities Administrators Association came out with a statement that said seven out of ten-day traders would end up losing all of their money.

In 2000, changes to the SOES were made to get rid of advantages for day traders, but then a stock market collapse came. After the dot-com bubble burst, many day traders became frightened or bankrupt and ran to different careers. The crazy frontier ways of day trading came to an end in 2008, as well as people who hope to get rich quickly. Now there are more professional day traders that work with diligence and care as if it were any other job. Take a step towards day trading In theory, anybody could be a pro football player, but in reality, there are a few people that have the right skill set for that sport. The same goes for day traders. The best traders need to have certain traits and have certain resources for them to be successful. Here are some of the most important things:

- Market knowledge and experience – To be successful with day trading, you are going to have to have some knowledge of market fundamentals. The most successful day traders are people who have experience in investing and in trading. They also make sure that they research things before they jump in.

- Capital – It may seem like a cliché, but "It takes money to make money," and this is extremely true when talking about day traders. A lot of traders will choose to borrow money, known as leverage, that they use to make their trades. Leverage tends to be riskier. Others make sure they have their capital saved before they trade.

- Business plan – When you choose to start day trading, you become a business owner, and this means you need a business plan. This plan should address your long and short-term goals, target markets, metrics, trading days and hours, reporting, business needs, tax considerations, and capital investment

- Discipline – Day traders have to avoid buying and selling based on their emotions. They understand how they should work with risk capital, they make sure they follow their limit and stop orders, to keep losses low, and they close out at the end of every business day.

- Technology – Day trading has to be done through electronic communication networks. You have to have use of a high-speed connection and a reliable computer to access the internet. A lot of traders will use a PC that has control over two monitors, a Wi-Fi connection on a laptop, a DSL backup, a clone computer, and cable broadband. They also have analytical software to control their accounts, research trades, perform trades, and receive information.

If a person decides to start day trading without having access to the necessary resources, they will most likely fail. If they do end up succeeding, they will most likely encounter a large learning curve. Once they gain experience, traders will either end up becoming a professional with an institution, or they will work by themselves. Either way, it is a full-time commitment.

Trading Secrets

As hard as day trading may seem, it becomes a lot easier once you learn a few rules and strategies about the way the market moves. Here are ten secrets that will help you to become a better day trader.

1. **Only trade with money you can afford to lose.**

A great trader will make sure to set aside some risk capital and will set aside a lot of money for long-term goals and retirement. Larger amounts of money should be invested for longer durations and in a more conservative fashion. It's not forbidden to use it when day trading, but you have to make sure that you have very favorable odds.

2. **Don't risk a large amount of capital on a single trade.**

Every day you should take the time to set a certain amount of your daily budget for each trade you plan on making. This is going to depend on the amount of money you have set aside to invest. Otherwise, you could end up missing out on some great opportunities.

3. Never Limit Yourself to Just Stocks.

Futures, options, and Forex are all asset options that will provide you with volatility and liquidity just like stocks will, which means they are great for day trading. A lot of the time, one of these options is going to give you an appealing opportunity when the stock market isn't doing very well.

4. Learn from previous experiences, but never second-guess yourself

Every day trader is going to experience a loss, so don't get upset with yourself when a trade ends up not working the way you thought it would. All you have to do is make sure you follow all of your rules and make sure you make no mistakes.

5. Keep an eye out for imbalanced supply and demand.

Like all things in life, if the supply is almost exhausted, and there are a lot of buyers, the price is going to end up going up. If there is a lot of supply, but not enough buyers that are interested, the price is going to go down.

6. **Have a target price before you start your day**.

Before you start to buy a stock, figure what profit is the most acceptable and then a stop-loss if your trade starts to go south. You have to stick to these choices once you make them. This will make sure you don't become greedy and will, more importantly, limit losses.

6. **Set a risk-reward ratio of 3:1 once you set targets.**

One of the most important things is to make sure you have a good risk-reward ratio. This will make sure that you receive big wins and small losses.

Chapter 1

How to Trade Options on Robinhood

What is Robinhood?

To put it simply, Robinhood is an online stock brokerage app for your smartphone. Robinhood differs from other stock trading apps like E*TRADE or TDAmeritrade. The major difference is that instead of charging 5-10 dollars commission on every trade plus an additional fee, Robinhood lets you make all your trades for free. They never charge you any commissions or fees, ever. This one simple difference opens up a lot of options for everyday people that were previously only available to the rich. Robinhood even gives away free shares of stocks like Apple, Microsoft, Ford, Sirius XM radio just for downloading their app.

When and Why to use Robinhood

Robinhood is still a new company. Using their app, you don't get the benefits of having your stocks in an IRA or Roth IRA. I wouldn't suggest using it to hold your life savings. What Robinhood is good for is starting a stock portfolio from nothing and building it with as little cost as possible to sizeable amounts, then transfer to an IRA or Roth IRA for long-term benefits. In our series, we will be using Robinhood to make more short-term trades to maximize growth in less than 5 years.

Downloading the app and getting your first free share of stock

Robinhood will give you a free share of stock just for downloading the app and opening an account. The accounts are free to open, so it won't cost you anything to open one. All you have to do is download the app using a referral link like this one CLICK HERE TO DOWNLOAD THE ROBINHOOD APP AND GET YOUR FIRST FREE STOCK. Enter your name and information to open an account. Then look under the menu select Free Stocks. On this page, you will see a link in the top right corner saying PAST INVITES click on this link to claim your free stock. You can also see a list of all the free stocks you receive here. Robinhood will give you 1 free share of a stock drawn at random from their inventory for every person you refer to using their app.

Watch list and Search functions

Robinhood has a watch list just like any other stock trading platform allowing you to track the price movements of your favorite stocks. It comes preloaded with some of the most popular stocks like Facebook, Apple, Google, and Amazon.

While you can trade these stocks on Robinhood, they are rather expensive anywhere from $100 to $1000. We will focus on using the search function to find stocks that are more affordable for beginners and adding them to our watch list. Robinhood does not suggest stocks for you to buy, and they don't have a list of all the stocks available. So, as far as finding stocks that you want to buy, you're pretty much on your own. You can search for stock tips and things like that on Google to find companies likely to go up in price and get the symbols for those companies like Facebook is FB, and Apple is AAPL.

Once you see the symbol for a company that you like to go to the Robinhood app and click on the little magnifying glass in the top right corner. Type in the symbol you found, and you will see the company come up.

From here, you will see a little circle with a plus symbol inside. You can click on this symbol to add a company to your watch list. Or, you can click on the name of the company for more details about the stock like price, volume, avg volume, market cap, dividend ratios, and so forth.

Buying your first stock

By now I'm sure you're ready to get started buying and selling the stock for a profit. I suggest you start small and work your way up. Find a stock you can afford and add it to your watch list. On your watch list, click on the stock you want to buy, and the details page will come up. At the bottom of the page, there is a button that will say trade or buy. Click on this button to start the buy order. Robinhood will automatically bring up the form to place a market order. Type in how many shares you want to buy and click send. You need to know that when using a market order, Robinhood may purchase the stock at up to a 5% higher price than the current market price. To buy stocks at a specific price, you need to use a limit order. You can change the order type by clicking on the link in the top right corner of the trading screen.

Market and Limit orders what are they used for

Market orders tell Robinhood that you want to vend this stock at whatever the market price is regardless of if it goes up or down. If you put in an order to buy shares, Robinhood will automatically purchase available shares up to 5% over the current market price. Anything more than 5%, and will not complete the order. Or, if you place an order to sell, it will sell at whatever the current market price is even if it drops rapidly. A limit order tells Robinhood that you want to vend this stock but only if it is available at a specific price. If you use the link in the top right corner of the trading screen to change the order type to a limit order, Robinhood will prompt you to enter the exact price you are about to pay for that stock, and it will only complete the order if it is available at the price you enter or lower. Or if you're selling, you will be prompted to enter the minimum amount your willing to vend for, and it will only be completed when the price reaches that point or greater.

Stop-loss and stop-limit orders what are they used for

A stop-loss order is an order to vend a stock if it reaches a specific price point. This type of order is your safety net, and we will be using it a lot later in our series to minimize risk. If you switch your order type to this, it will prompt you to enter a price. If you are buying, you want to enter the price you want to buy at, and when the stock reaches that price or

higher your order will be converted to an order. If you are selling you, want to enter a price so that if the price of the stock falls below that point, your order will be converted to

an order. This is useful because it allows you to set up a safety net, so you don't have to be watching your stocks constantly to avoid a loss. For example, you buy a stock for $5.00. You set your stop loss to sell if the price falls below $4.95.

If the price goes up, you will continue to hold the stock and make money. If the price drops below $4.95, your order will convert to order and sell the stock to avoid further losses. A stop-limit order is an order to vend a stock at a specific price point. But will convert to a limit order when the stock hits that point. You must set two price points for a stop-limit order. One price point at which to convert the order and another at which to limit order. What this allows you to do is to create in which to buy the stock. For example, you think if a certain stock breaks past its 52-week high, it will get a bump from lots of people hoping it will continue to go up. But once that initial wave of buyers is over, the volume will go back to normal, and it will go back down some then continue to rise slowly. Let's say the stock is $8 per share. The 52-week high is $10 per share. You place a stop-limit order with the converted price at $10 per share and the limit at $15 per share. A large hedge fund buys into the stock and places a large order for millions of shares at the end of the day. The stock skyrockets to $20 in after-hours trading. You're using a free account, so your orders can't execute after-market hours. In the morning, when the markets open, the big players have already completed their orders. The price is still $20 but drops because no small investors are willing to pay such a hefty price. Had you used a stop-loss order, you would have purchased the stock at an exorbitant price, and then it would fall back down. But by using a stop-limit order you won't buy any shares unless the price is below $15.

Chapter 2

Binary Trading Options

Trading alternatives are accessible in a few exceptional shapes. The dial type is the parallel dial. Paired dialing is an alternative that pays off at a predefined time inside a foreordained range. Concerning the current period, there can be extensive adaptability, from short to long. 60-second double alternatives function as a momentary exchanging procedure or convention. This sort of alternative permits the broker to anticipate the bearing of the stock cost in a brief timeframe, incorrectly one moment.

Exchanging this kind of double choice includes looking at a diagram with current stock value information. The individual at that point chooses whether he figures the stock cost will rise or fall toward the finish of the one minute.

Since the time related to this sort of exchange is so short, these exchanges happen at an exceptionally high recurrence. This requires the individual to settle on estimating choices and related issues inside seconds in a profoundly compacted period.

Since exchanging through this kind of paired methodology is rapid, one ought not to hop into these sorts of exercises without finishing the instructive procedure. The most ideal approach to set up an individual to take an interest in this sort of exchanging with 60 seconds alternatives is to set up and utilize a demo account.

A demo account gives an individual diverse exchanging situation. Likewise, a demo account is instrumental in helping an individual settle on powerful exchanging choices seconds if important.

One ought to never take part in this sort of genuine cash twofold exchanging until one has aced the procedure through a demo account. To what extent it takes relies upon the individual. A few people can without much of a stretch control a demo account quicker than others.

An individual who has aced a demo record and afterward exchanges for genuine cash can make a lot of cash in this procedure. Be that as it may, this sort of alternatives exchanging - similarly as with a wide range of choices exchanging - presents dangers. In this way, one should be cautious when putting resources into these kinds of choices. Good karma and shrewd exchanging!

Exchange Futures Options to Achieve High Returns

Twofold alternatives exchanging is a sort of web-based exchanging that centers around the heading of items, stocks, prospects, records, and monetary forms. It's like forex exchanging by exchanging wares, regardless of whether they rise or fall. With this kind of exchange, you have an exceptionally effective and simple approach to rake in boatloads of cash in an hour or half a month, contingent upon your decision of exchanging time.

When exchanging fates, financial specialists bring in cash by expecting changes in ware costs. Products that are exchanged on a stock trade are the equivalent paying little heed to their source. Alternatives prospects are, in this way, protections that give their holders the option to buy item fates, for example, gold, paper, or outside cash at a set cost.

There are two fundamental kinds of alternatives exchanging prospects to pay special mind to calls and puts. You possibly purchase a call choice on the off chance that you figure the base cost of fates will increment. For instance, on the off chance that you expect corn fates to improve, purchase the choice to purchase corn. The inverse is the business approach. You possibly purchase a call alternative on the off chance that you think the base prospects' cost will drop. For instance, in the event that you anticipate that the eventual fate of soybeans should decrease, purchase a soybean alternative. You should follow through on the cost when buying this sort of choice. The term utilized at the choice cost is known as the premium. You can think about the alternatives as a wager.

The more drawn out the shot, the less expensive the setting. Then again, the surer you are, the costlier it will be.

The strike cost is the value you can purchase or sell from the fundamental fates contract. It is basic to recognize prospects' alternatives and fates contracts. A prospect alternative is a money-related instrument that gives the dealer the option to purchase a fates contract for a particular thing. Conversely, a prospect's contract is a legally binding commitment to buy the item itself, in a predetermined amount, at a predefined cost, and at a predefined time.

You don't need to be such an incredible money-related master when exchanging double alternatives. In contrast to different sorts of exchange, where you have to deal with complex measurements and have classified data, all you have to know is whether you figure the cost of benefits will rise or fall. The degree of hazard is likewise decreased during exchanging.

When you have an agreement, you know precisely how much capital you are gambling and the amount you can win. At whatever point you exchange prospects' choices, you are certain because you don't need to think of a

leave technique. All things considered, the length of the agreement is resolved before entering the exchange.

Albeit probably the most broadly utilized money-related instruments today are one of the more usually utilized, they can be confused and convey an unimaginably high hazard.

Then again, alternative exchanging methodologies can make exchanges more secure. Alternatives are presumably the most adaptable exchanging apparatuses accessible and are additionally amazing and flexible devices that you can use as a stock merchant to quantify hazard and increment benefits.

Financial specialist Notice of Binary Options Trading

Any place you are, speculations appear to be the most recent news. You've most likely heard it on TV and the Internet since choices exchanging is something that numerous individuals concoct. Individuals who think they are happy to put resources into something that can bring a superior return should initially plan. Exchanging is energizing; however, you should know more before you get included, particularly if alternative exchanging is another and obscure idea for you.

Assess What You Want

Choices exchanging is accessible in an assortment of sizes, so it's ideal to realize who to concentrate on. Ordinary alternatives can be a potential decision, and it is something that numerous individuals pick. All installment understandings lapse on the third Friday or Saturday, contingent upon which showcase you exchange. Parallel alternatives permit you to purchase and foresee hourly lapse times.

The two stages are legitimate exchanging configurations, and it is dependent upon you to consider what might be a superior arrangement. Customers who are anxious and may need quicker outcomes may decide to exchange parallel alternatives, as this can prompt quicker payouts.

Hypothetically, somebody can exchange now and get installments a couple of hours after the fact. For the individuals who need to have time, attempt the standard settings, and sit tight for the outcomes on the chose to date.

Realize Business Styles

Alternatives exchanging is a venture step, and you have to realize the accessible exchanging styles. You have to acknowledge what it resembles to design your best course of action. For instance, the twofold choice has two exchanging styles: American and European. European-style exchanging follows through on-off if the cost on the assigned day is above or beneath the concurred level. In a U.S. exchange, installment

can be made if the sum surpasses the concurred level whenever by the allocated date. When you realize these two exchanging styles, you ought to figure out which one better suits your exchanging style.

Discover a Dealer

Numerous venture organizations routinely exchange choices, so, it might be simpler for customers to discover them. Double choices can be all the more testing because numerous organizations that offer it are online.

Clients considering parallel alternatives should then scan the Internet for business. In the pursuit box, enter "choices parallel organizations" to see the professional resources and rundown of sites you see.

Peruse the particular business states of twofold alternatives and discover how they acknowledge customers. A few areas may expect you to open a record with them and give a Visa number before you can make buys.

Before doing whatever else, check the foundation of these organizations with purchaser business gatherings and government offices. This progression should help guarantee that the online choices exchange is legitimate and lawful. Additionally, ensure that the organization you pick has a protection strategy.

Locate the most reasonable exchanging organization and style of your decision. If a business or corporate

style appears to suit your objectives, check out it. The excellence of exchanging is that a potential broker is hanging tight for a potential payout. This may imply that the sooner you exchange, the more without further ado you will get installment.

Is a Binary Option Suitable for You?

Exchanging twofold alternatives or advanced choices, which are here and there alluded to, give merchants considerably more adaptability and decision than traditional kinds of choices.

This kind of exchanging permits brokers to exchange an assortment of budgetary instruments, including stocks, wares, monetary forms, and that's only the tip of the iceberg. Computerized alternatives exchanging offers dealers the chance to acquire 60-80% of exchanges a brief timeframe, even as a rule in 60 minutes.

The benefits of this exchanging offer are that exchanging is a straightforward procedure, and there is constrained hazard contrasted with exchanging regular choices. Dealers must be directed as far as a value bearing to exploit. Double alternatives are given 24 hours every day, and the dealer can pick diverse periods for each exchange. The hazard is pre-decided and decided with the goal that dealers know precisely what the benefit or misfortune will be in a given exchange.

Advanced choices are significantly less hazardous than different kinds of exchanging, predominantly Forex, because they don't include any influence or a "stop-misfortune" relationship. Dealers don't need to stress that exchanges will contradict their position and endure gigantic misfortunes. The hazard is constantly constrained to the sum put resources into every exchange. This gives dealers the adaptability to exchange even in the steadiest okay markets.

Benefits are made with regards to cash from one cross-exchange. Brokers don't need to stress over the value arriving at a specific point to make a benefit.

Dealers never need to stress over exchanging paired alternatives on edge. The base record expected to begin exchanging is a lot littler than what is required to buy in different markets, for example, Forex, wares, and stocks. What can be exchanged is practically unhindered. Alternatives are given on the most well-known instruments, for example, monetary forms, gold, oil, and products.

Chapter 3

Options Day Trading Rules for Success

There is more to options day trading than just having a style or a strategy. If that was all it took, then you could just adopt those that are proven to work and just stick with them. Yes, options day trading styles and strategy are important but they are not the end-all-be-all of this career.

The winning factor is the options day trader himself or herself. You are the factor that determines whether or not you will win or lose in this career. Only taking the time to develop your expertise, seeking guidance when necessary, and being dedicated allows a person to move from a novice options day trader to an experienced one that is successful and hitting his or her target goals.

To develop into the options day trader you want to be, being disciplined is necessary. There are options day trading rules that can help you develop that necessary discipline. You will make mistakes. Every beginner in any niche does and even experienced options day traders are human and thus, have bad days too.

Knowing common mistakes helps you avoid many of these mistakes and takes away much of the guesswork. Having rules to abide by helps you avoid these mistakes as well.

Below, I have listed 11 rules that every options day trader must know. Following them is entirely up to you but know that they are proven to help beginner options day traders turn into winning options day traders.

Rule for Success #1 – Have Realistic Expectations

It is sad to say that many people who enter the options trading industry are doing so to make a quick buck. Options trading is not a get-rich-quick scheme. It is a reputable career that has made many people rich but that is only because these people have put in the time, effort, study, and dedication to learning the craft and mastering it. Mastery does not happen overnight and beginner options day traders need to be prepared for that learning curve and to have the fortitude to stick with day trading options even when it becomes tough.

Losses are also part of the game. No trading style or strategy will guarantee gains all the time. The best options traders have a winning percentage of about 80% and a losing average of approximately 20%. That is why an options day trader needs to be a good money manager and a good risk manager. Be prepared for eventual losses and be prepared to minimize those losses.

Rule for Success #2 – Start Small to Grow a Big Portfolio

Caution is the name of the game when you just get started with day trading options. Remember that you are still learning options trading and developing an understanding of the financial market. Do not jump the gun even if you are eager. After you have practiced paper trading, start with smaller options positions and steadily grow your standing as you get a lay of the options day trading land. This strategy allows you to keep your losses to a minimum and to develop a systematic way of entering positions.

Rule for Success #3 – Know Your Limits

You may be tempted to trade as much as possible to develop a winning monthly average but that strategy will have the opposite effect and land you with a losing average. Remember that every options trader needs careful consideration before that contract is set up. Never overtrade and tie up your investment fund.

Rule for Success #4 – Be Mentally, Physically and Emotionally Prepared Every Day

This is a mentally, physically, and emotionally tasking career and you need to be able to meet the demands of this career. That means keeping your body, mind, and heart in good health at all times. Ensure that you schedule time for self-care every day. That can be as simple as taking the time to read for recreation to having an elaborate self-care routine carved out in the evenings.

Not keeping your mind, heart, and head in optimum health means that they are more likely to fail you. Signs that you need to buckle up and care for yourself more diligently include being constantly tired, being short-tempered, feeling preoccupied, and being easily distracted.

To ensure you perform your best every day, here a few tasks that you need to perform:

- Get the recommended amount of sleep daily. This is between 7 and 9 hours for an adult.

- Practice a balanced diet. The brain and body need adequate nutrition to work their best. Include fruits, complex carbs, and veggies in this diet and reduce the consumption of processed foods.

- Eat breakfast lunch and dinner every day. Fuel your mind and body with the main meals. Eating a healthy breakfast is especially important because it helps set the tone for the rest of the day.

- Exercise regularly. Being inactive increases your risk of developing chronic diseases like heart disease, certain cancers, and other terrible health consequences. Adding just a few minutes of exercise to your daily routine not only reduces those risks but also allows your brain to function better, which is a huge advantage for an options day trader.

- Drink alcohol in moderation or not at all.

- Stop smoking.

- Reduce stress contributors in your environment.

Rule for Success #5 – Do Your Homework Daily

Get up early and study the financial environment before the market opens and look at the news. This allows you to develop a daily options trading plan. The process of analyzing the financial climate before the market opens is called pre-market preparation. It is a necessary task that needs to be performed every day to asset competition and to align your overall strategy with the short-term conditions of that day.

An easy way to do this is to develop a pre-market checklist. An example of a pre-market checklist includes but is not limited to:

- Checking the individual markets that you frequently trade options in or plan to trade options in to evaluate support and resistance.

- Checking the news to assess whether events that could affect the market developed overnight.

- Assessing what other options traders are doing to determined volume and competition.

- Determining what safe exits for losing positions are.

- Considering the seasonality of certain markets are some as affected by the day of the week, the month of the year, etc.

Rule for Success #6 – Analyze Your Daily Performance

To determine if the options day trading style and strategies that you have adopted are working for you, you need to track your performance. At the most basic, this needs to be done daily because you are trading options daily. This will allow you to notice patterns in your profit and loss. This can lead to you determining the why and how of these gains and losses. These determinations lead to fine-tuning your daily processes for maximum returns. These daily performance reviews allow you to also make determinations on the long-term activity of your options day trading career.

Rule for Success #7 – Do Not Be Greedy

If you are fortunate enough to make a 100% return on your investment, do not be greedy and try to reap more benefits from the position. You might have the position turn on you and you can lose everything. When and if such a rare circumstance happens to you, sell your position and take the profits.

Rule for Success #8 – Pay Attention to Volatility

Volatility speaks to how likely a price change will occur over a specific amount of time on the financial market. Volatility can work for an options day trader or against the options day trader. It all depends on what the options day trader is trying to accomplish and what his or her current position is.

Many external factors affect volatility and such factors include the economic climate, global events, and news reports. Strangles and straddles strategies are great for use in volatile markets.

There are different types of volatility and they include:

- Price volatility, which describes how the price of an asset increases or decreases based on the supply and demand of that asset.

- Historical volatility, which is a measure of how an asset has performed over the last 12 months.

- Implied volatility, which is a measure of how an asset will perform in the future.

Rule for Success #9 – Use the Greeks

Greeks are a collection of measures that provide a gauge of an option's price sensitivity concerning other factors. Each Greek is represented by a letter from the Greek alphabet. These Greeks use complex formulas to be determined but they are the system that option pricing is based on. Even though these calculations can be complex, they can be done quickly and efficiently so that options day traders can use them as a method of advancing their trades for the most profitable position. The 5 Greeks that are used in options trading are:

Delta

This Greek defines the price relationship between an option and its associated asset. Delta is a direct translation of a change in the price of the associated asset into the changing of the price of an option. Call options deltas to range from 1 to 0 while put options deltas range from 0 to -1. An example of a delta as it relates to a call option is a call option with a delta of 0.5. If the price of the associated asset increases by $200, then the price of the call option will increase by $100.

Vega

This Greek is a measure of the sensitivity of the price of an option to the implied volatility of the associated asset. Option prices are greatly impacted by the volatility of the associated asset's prices because greater volatility translates into a higher chance that the price of the associated asset will reach or surpass the strike price on or before the expiration date of the option.

Theta

This Greek is a measure of the sensitivity of the price of an option to the time decay of the value of the option. Time decay describes the rate of deterioration in the value of the contract because of the passage of time. The closer the expiration date becomes; the more time decay accelerates because the time left to gain a profit narrow. Therefore, the longer it takes to reach an options' expiration date, the more value this option has because it has a longer period to gain the trader a profit. The theta is a negative figure because time is always a diminishing factor. This figure becomes increasingly negative the closer the expiration date becomes.

Gamma

These Greek measures the rate of change of the delta of an option. At its most basic, it tells the likelihood of an option reaching or surpassing the strike price.

Rho

This Greek is a measure of an option's value compared to changes in interest rate. Options with longer expiration dates are more likely to be affected by changes in interest rates.

Chapter 4

Creating Your Own Day Trading Strategy

As you start to get more into day trading, you may decide to develop your own strategy. There are a lot of great trading strategies that are out there so far, but there may be some market conditions or other situations where you need to be able to develop your strategy. Or, after trying out a few different things, you end up finding a new strategy, or a combination of strategies, that ends up working out the best.

Over time, you must find your place inside the market. As you go through, you may even find that you would rather be more like a swing trader rather than a day trader just because of the available different methods. The good news is, there is a market for any kind of trader, and there are a million types of strategies that you can use based on your personal preferences along the way.

Before you jump into the market as a beginner with your trading strategy, you must start by picking one of the strategies that are in this guidebook (or another proven strategy that you have researched). You need to have some time to try out a strategy and tread through the market a bit before you start coming up with your strategy. Even if you have invested in the stock market before, you will find that working with day trading is completely different compared to some of the other methods available, and you do not want to pick a strategy that may have worked with one of your other trades, but will make you fail miserably with day trading.

It is all about spending some time in the market and getting familiar with the market. You will want to get familiar with how the day trading market works, how to recognize good stocks, and so on before you make a good strategy that can help you. After spending some time in the market, working with one or two strategies that you like, you will be able to learn the patterns that you like and what to watch out for, and it becomes so much easier to make a strategy that will work. But no matter where you are as a trader, it is so important that every trader has a strategy of some sort to help them get started. It is so easy for beginners to just pick out a stock and then start trading, without having a plan in place at all. This is a dangerous thing to work with. It pretty much leaves the decisions up to your emotions, and we all know how dangerous this can be when you are first starting. You should never leave your trades up to emotions; this will make you stay in the market too long or leave the market too early, and you will end up losing money.

In addition, you need to pick one strategy, whether it is one from this guidebook or one that you made up on your own, and then you need to stick with that strategy. Learn all of the rules that go with that strategy, how to make that strategy work for you, and exactly how you should behave at different times in the market with that strategy. Even if it ends up leading you to a bad trade (remember that any type of strategy and even the best traders will end up with a bad trade on occasion), you will stick it out until the trade is done. You can always switch strategies in between trades, but it is never a good idea to switch your strategy once you are already in the market.

Switching strategies can seem tempting when you are a beginner in the market. You may see that things are going south or may realize once you are in the market that you should have done a different strategy from the beginning. But as you look through some of the strategies that are in this guidebook, you probably notice that they are a bit different, and they need some different requirements before you can get in and out of the trade. Switching in the middle is not going to work and will lead to an automatic loss.

The most important thing that you can remember when you become a day trader is that all traders will fail at some point. Many beginners will fail because they do not take the time to learn how to properly day trade or they let their emotions get in the way of making smart decisions. But even advanced traders will have times when they will fail and lose money as well. The market is not always the most reliable thing in the world. Even when you are used to reading the charts and looking at the market, there will be times when it does not act as expected and a trader will lose out. Or the advanced trader may choose to try out a new strategy, and it does not work that well for them.

There will be times when you will lose money, and this can be hard to handle for a lot of beginners. This is also why you need to consider how much you can afford to lose on a trade before you enter the market. You do not want to go all out on your first trade because it is likely you will fail and lose that money or maybe more depending on the trade.

If you are worried about getting started in the market or you want to mess around and try out a few of the strategies ahead of time to see how they work, especially if you are using one of your strategies, then you should consider working with a simulator. Sometimes you will be able to get one of these from your broker to try out and experiment with the market, and sometimes you may have to pay a bit from another site to use this simulator. However, this can be a valuable tool that will help you to try out different things, make changes, and get a little familiarity in the market before you invest your actual money. As a beginner, if you have access to one of these simulators, it is worth your time to give it a try.

Picking your trade based on the time of day

Before we move on, we will take a look at which types of strategies seem to work the best at different times of the day. As you get into the market, you will notice that each period of the day will be different and some patterns seem to show up over time with them. We will work with

three times of day, the open, the mid-day, and the close. If you want to be successful with day trading, it is not a good idea to use the same strategy at all three times of the day because these strategies will not be successful at all times of the day. The best traders will figure out what time of day they get the most profitable trades and then they will make some adjustments to their strategies and their trading to fit them into these profitable times.

First, let's talk about the open. This period will last about an hour and a half, starting at 9:30 in the morning on New York Time. This is a busy time of the day because people are joining the market for the first time or they are adjusting based on how their stocks had done overnight. Because this time is so busy, it can also be a profitable period if you play the game right. It is a good idea to increase the size of your trades during this time and do more of them because you are more likely to make some good money during this time. The best strategies to use during the open will be the VWAP trades and the Bull Flag Momentum.

The next session is the mid-day session, and this will start at 11 in the morning and go for about four hours. This is a slow time in the market, and it is considered one of the more dangerous times to trade during the day. There is not going to be much liquidity or volume in the market. Even a smaller order will make a stock move quite a bit during this time, so you need to watch the market if you are holding onto your stocks. It is more likely that you will be stopped with unexpected and strange moves during this period.

It is common for many traders, both beginners and those who are more advanced, to have a lot of trouble during the mid-day. Many decide that it is not the best idea to work in the market during this time. But if you do decide to trade, it is important to keep the stops tight and also to lower your share size.

You should also be picky about the risk and reward ratio during this time. You will find that new traders will often do their overtrading during this time, and it may be best to simply avoid trading during this period altogether.

If you do decide to trade during the mid-day, it is best to watch the stocks as closely as possible, get some things ready for a close, and always be very careful about any trading decisions that you try to do. You will find that support or resistance trades, moving average, VWAP, and reversal strategies work well during the mid-day.

And finally, there is the close, which starts at 3 in the afternoon and goes for about an hour. These stocks are considered more directional, so it is best to stick with those that are going either down or up during this last hour. It is possible to raise the tier size compared to what it was at in mid-day, but you do not want to go as high as you were at open. You will find that the prices at closing are often going to reflect what the traders on Wall Street think the value of the stocks is. These traders have stayed out of the market during the day, but they have been closely watching things so that they can get in and dominate what happens during the last little bit of trading.

It is also common to see that many market professionals will sell their stocks at this time and take the profits because they do not want to hold onto the trades overnight. As a day trader, you will be one of these professionals because you need to sell all of your stocks on the same day to be a day trader.

Chapter 5

How Options Prices are Determined

O ptions prices are determined in part by the price of the underlying stock. But options prices are also influenced by the time left to expiration and some other factors. We are going to go over all the different ways that the price of a given option can change and what will be behind the changes. It's important to have a firm grasp of these concepts so that you don't go into options as a naïve beginning trader.

Market price of shares

The largest factor that impacts the price of an option is the price of the investment known as the stock that is behind the option. However, it's not a 1-1 relationship. The amount of influence from the underlying stock is going to change with time. Furthermore, it depends on whether the option is in the money, at the money, or out of the money. The fraction of the options price that is due to the price of the underlying stock is called the options' intrinsic value.

If an option can be the same as the market pricing or not be comparatively favored, it has zero intrinsic value. An option would have to be priced in the money to have any intrinsic value.

- For a call option, if the market price is lower than the strike price or the same, the option will have no pricing at all from the intrinsic value. If the share price is higher than the price used to trade shares via the option, the option will have intrinsic value.

- For a put option, if the share price is at or above the strike price, the option will have zero intrinsic value. If the share price is below the strike price, then the option will have some value from the stock. This is called intrinsic value.

However, to confuse matters, even when an option is at or out of the money, the price of the underlying stock has some influence that can change the value of the option. The amount of influence that the market price of the item known as the stock has on the price of the option is given by a quantity that is called delta. You can read the value for delta by looking at the data for any option that you are interested in trading. It is given as a decimal value ranging from 0 to 1 for call options, and it's given as a negative value for put options. The reason it's given as a negative value for put options is that this reflects the fact that if the stock price is found to increase, the price of a put option will be reduced. In contrast, if the stock price declines, the value of the put option will increase. It's an inverse relationship, and thus, the delta is negative for put options.

To understand how this will play out, let's look at a specific example. Suppose that we have a $100 option. That is, the strike price is set to $100. If the price of the underlying stock is $105, the delta for the call option is 0.77.

That means that if the dollar value of the stock increases by $1, the value of the option will rise by approximately 77 cents. This is a per-share price change. So, for the option that you are trading, there are 100 underlying shares.

So, a 77 cents price rise would increase the value of the option by $77.

For a put option with the same strike price, the option would be out of the money, because the share price is higher than the strike price. In this case, for the put option, the delta is given as -0.23. That means that the put option would lose approximately $23 if the share price went up by $1. On the other hand, if the share price dropped by $1, the put option would gain $23.

The intrinsic value of the call option described in this theoretical exercise would be $5 per share. The total cost of the option would be $6.06 per share, reflecting the fact that the call option has $1.06 in extrinsic value. In contrast, the put option has zero intrinsic value. It has almost the same extrinsic value, however, at $1.03.

I have used a 45-day time frame before expiration for this exercise. Options prices are governed by mathematical formulas, so it's possible to make estimates of what the option price is going to be ahead of time. Some many calculators and spreadsheets are available free online for this purpose.

Now, let's say that instead, the share price was $95 so that the call option was out of the money and the put option was in the money. In this case, the call option has zero intrinsic value, and it has a $0.94 extrinsic value, so the option would be worth $94. Delta has switched, but not exactly. In this case, for the call option, the delta is 0.25. If the share price rose to

$96, with everything else unchanged, the price of the call option would rise to $1.21 per share. This illustrates that you can still earn profits from cheaper out-of-the-money options.

If the share price stayed at $95, the put option would have a delta of -0.75. Notice that if we take the absolute value and add the delta for the call and the put option, they sum up to 1.0.

So, if you see an option of the call type that has a strike that is lower than the market price, with a delta given by say 0.8, that means the put option with the same strike price and expiration date will have a delta of -0.20.

Delta does more than give you the prediction of changes in the underlying share price and price movements of the option. It also gives you a (rough) estimate of the probability to expire in the money for the contract known as an option.

If you sell to open, you don't want the option to expire in the money. Therefore, you are probably going to sell options that have a small delta. On the other hand, if you buy to open, you want the option to go in the money, if it isn't already. So, you would buy an option with a higher delta.

If we say that a given call option has a delta of 0.66, this indicates if we see changes such that the underlying stock price rises by $1, the price of the option on a per-share basis will rise by $0.66. But it also tells us that there is a 66% chance that this option will expire in a positive condition, that is it will be in the money.

Something else you need to know is that the delta is dynamic. If the price of a share increases on the market, the delta rises for the call option and gets smaller in magnitude for the put option. A declining share price will have the opposite effect.

The amount that delta will change is given by another "Greek" – gamma. Most beginning traders probably aren't going to be too worried about gamma, what we've described so far is all you need to know to enter into effective options trades. But gamma will tell you the variation in the value of the delta with a change in stock price. So, if gamma is 0.03, this means that a $1 rise in the stock price will increase delta by 0.03 for a call option. The inverse relationship holds for a put option.

If an option is at the money, the delta is going to be about 0.50 for a call option and -0.50 for a put option. That makes sense, if the strike price is equal to the share price on the market, there is a 50% probability that the market price will move below the strike price, and there is a 50% probability that the market cost of shares will move above the strike price.

Implied Volatility

One of the most important characteristics of options after considering delta and time decay is the amount a stock price varies with time. Volatility will give you an idea of how will the price swings of stock are. If you look at a stock chart, I am sure that you are used to seeing the price go up and down a lot giving a largely jagged curve. The more that it fluctuates, and the bigger the fluctuations in price, the higher the volatility. Of course, everything is relative and so you can't say that any stock has an "absolute" level of volatility. What is done is the volatility for the entire market is calculated, and then the volatility of a stock is compared to the volatility of the market as a whole. When looking at the stocks themselves, this is given by a quantity called beta.

If the stock generally moves with the stock market at large, beta is positive. If beta is 1.0, that means that it has the same volatility as the entire market. That is a stock with average volatility.

If beta is less than 1.0, then the stock doesn't have much volatility. The amount below 1.0 tells you how much less volatile the stock is in comparison to the market as a whole. So, if the beta is given as 0.7, this means that the stock is 30% less volatile than the market average.

If beta is greater than 1.0, then the stock is more volatile than the average. If you see a stock with a beta of 1.42, that means the stock is 42% more volatile than the average for the market. If beta is negative, that means the stock, on average, moves against the market. When the market goes up, it goes down and vice versa. Most stocks don't have a negative beta but they are not hard to find either.

Volatility is a dynamic quantity, so when you look it up, you are looking at a snapshot of the volatility at that given moment. Of course, under most circumstances, it's not likely to change very much over short periods like a few weeks or a month. There are exceptions to this, including earnings season.

Implied volatility is a quantity that is given for options. Implied volatility is a measure of the coming volatility that the stock price is expected to see over the lifetime of the option (that is until the expiration date).

One of the things that make options valuable is the probability that the price of the stock will move in a direction that is favorable to the strike price. When an option goes in the money, or deeper in the money (that is the share price moves even higher relative to the strike price of a call, or lower relative to the strike price of a put), the value of the option can increase by a large margin.

Chapter 6

Tips for Day Trading Options

This is a much better and more successful strategy. Here are some helpful tips and advice that should guide you as you trade online in options.

1. The Price of Any Stock Can Move in 3 Basic Directions

These directions are up, down, and no movement at all. Depending on the kind of call that you have, you can leverage this movement to make a profit or at least avoid incurring losses.

Plenty of first-time traders and investors assume that prices of securities will go either up or down. However, this is the wrong school of thought because sometimes there is no movement at all in the price of stocks and shares. This is a very important fact in the world of options trading.

There are plenty of real-life, practical examples that show a particular stock or share which did not move significantly for quite a lengthy period. For instance, the KOL share traded within a $4 range for a total of 23 days. If you had invested money in either a call option or a put option through this stock, you would have lost money.

According to seasoned traders, chances of making a profit with a call or put option are hardly ever 50% but only 33%. This is likely because stock price movements are random. You will eventually realize that 33% of the time, stocks rise; 33% of the time, they dip in price; and another 33% of the time, they stay the same. Time will more often be your worst enemy if you have a long put or call option.

A purchase of a call option is usually with the hope that prices will go up. If prices do rise, then you will make a profit. At other times, the prices will remain the same or even fall. In such events, if you have an out-of-the-money call, the option will most likely expire, and you will lose your investment. If the price remains stagnant and you have an in-the-money option, then you will at least recoup some of the money you invested.

There will be sometimes when frustrations will engulf you. This is when you just sit and watch prices start to skyrocket just a couple of weeks after the options you purchased had expired. This is often an indicator that your strategy was not on point and you did not give it sufficient time. Even seasoned traders sometimes buy call options that eventually expire in a given month and then the stock prices rise sharply in the following month.

It is therefore advisable to purchase a longer-term call option rather than one that expires after a single month. Now, since stocks move in 3 general directions, it is assumed that close to 70% of options, traders with long call and put options suffer losses. On the other hand, this implies that 70% of options sellers make money. This is one of the main reasons why conservative options traders prefer to write or sell options.

2. Before Buying a Call or Put Option, Look at the Underlying Stock's Chart

You want to find out as much information as possible about the performance and worth of an underlying stock before investing in it.

You should, therefore, ensure that you take a serious look at the chart of the stock. This chart should indicate the performance of the stock in the last couple of days. The best is to look at a stock's performance in the last 30 and 90 days. You should also take a look at its last year's performance.

When you look at the charts, look at the movement of the shares and try and note any trends. Also, try and observe any general movement of the shares. Then answer a couple of questions. For instance, is the stock operating within a narrow range? Or is it bending upwards or downwards? Is this chart in tandem with your options trading strategy?

To identify the trend of a particular stock, try and draw a straight line along in the middle of the share prices. Then draw a line both above and below to indicate a channel of the general flow of the share.

Chart Readings and Buying Call Options

Let us assume that you wish to invest in a call option. Then you should ask yourself if the stock price is likely to rise and why. If you think that the stock will rise and trade at a higher level, then you may be mistaken, unless something drastic happens or new information becomes evident. New information can be a shareholders' meeting, impending earnings announcement, a new CEO, product launch, and so on.

If there is a chart showing the presence of support at lower prices and stock prices fall to that level, then it may be advisable to buy call options. The call option will be a great bet when prices are down because prices will very likely head back up. However, never allow greed to occupy your mind. When you see a profit, take and do not wait too long.

Chart Readings and Buying Put Options

Now, supposing the stock chart indicates a solid resistance at a higher price. If the stock is beginning to approach this higher level, then the price might begin to move in that direction as well. So as the price moves, expect to gain small but significant profits. Avoid greed, so anytime the stock price falls, simply move in and make some money.

Chart Readings for Purchase of Call and Put Options

Now, if your chart readings indicate that the shares are within the lower levels of their range, then it is likely that daily price changes will send it towards the middle of the range. If this is so, then you should move in and make a profit as soon as the price tends upwards. Even minor profits such as buying at $1 and selling at $1.15 mean a 15% profit margin.

3. Find Out the Breakeven Point Before Buying Your Options

Now, you need to identify a call option that you wish to invest in, especially after studying its performance on the market. Before buying, however, you should work out the breakeven point. To find this breakeven point, you will have to consider things such as the commissions charged and the bid spread.

You must be positive that the underlying stock of your options will move sufficiently to surpass the breakeven point and earn a tidy profit. You should, therefore, learn how to work out the breakeven point in an options trade.

Calculating the Breakeven Point

As an options trader, you need to know how to calculate and find the breakeven point. In options trading, there are 2 break-even points. With short-term options, you need to make use of the commission rates and bid spread to work out the breakeven point. This is if you intend to hold on to the options until their expiration date.

Now, if you are seeking short-term trade without holding on to the options, then find out the difference between the asking price and bid price. This difference is also known as the spread.

4. If You Are Dealing with Call and Put Options, Embrace the Underlying Stock's Trend

As an investor and trader in options, you need to consider the trend of the underlying stock as your friend. This means that you should not fight it. If the stock price is headed upwards, you should find a strategy that is in tandem with this movement. If you oppose it, you are unlikely to win.

Similarly, if the stock is on a downward trend, then do not oppose this movement but try and find a strategy that will accommodate this trend. You need to understand, however, that this saying is intended to guide you but is not necessarily a rule. This means that you apply it even while you consider all other factors. For instance, the major news may have an immediate effect on the price trend of a stock or shares.

As a trader, you should learn to jump successfully on a trend and follow the crowds rather than go to extremes and oppose it. Most amateurs who see an upward trend often think the stock is about to level out. However, the reality is that momentum is often considered a great thing by seasoned traders. Therefore, do not try and oppose the trend because you will surely lose. Instead, try and design a strategy that will accommodate the trend. In short, the trend is always your friend, do not resist, and momentum is truly great.

5. When Trading Options, Watch Out for Earnings Release Dates

Call and put options are generally expensive with the price increases significantly if there is an earnings release announcement looming. The reason is that the anticipation of very good or very bad earnings reports will likely affect the stock price. When this is an underlying stock in an options trade, then you should adjust your trades appropriately.

Once an earnings release has been made, then options prices will fall significantly. You need to also watch out very carefully for this. The prices will first go up just before the earnings release and then fall shortly thereafter. It is also possible for call options prices to dip despite earnings announcements. This may happen if the earnings announced are not as impressive as expected.

As an example, stocks such as Google may rise insanely during the earnings announcement week only to dip significantly shortly thereafter. Consider Apple shares that were trading at $450 at the markets. Call options with Apple as the underlying stock were trading at $460. However, the market had targeted a price of $480 within 3 days, which did not happen. This cost investors money. Such underlying assets are considered volatile due to the high increase in price, rapid drop shortly thereafter and related risk of losing money.

Additional Tips for Advanced Options Traders

One of the best pieces of advice for all advanced options traders specifically and all other traders, in general, is investing in education. Some of the most crucial trading techniques involve evaluating stocks, conducting fundamental analysis as well as performing technical analysis. You also need to be able to make decisions regarding the impending and future movement of a security.

Options can be risky, and time is always against you. As such, you should be able to predict and foretell as accurately as possible the impending and future direction of an individual stock and the overall trend of the market.

Advanced Stock Options

Stock options are very similar to futures contracts. They also closely resemble ordinary stocks. However, they are all inherently different. As such, options can be viewed as contracts. Therefore, anytime a trader deals in options, they are dealing in a contract referencing underlying security. This is basic information that all stock traders are aware of but is essential for refreshing the memory.

Chapter 7

Application on the Options Market

Very successful investor says that research makes all the difference not only in options trading but trading in general. The better resources you have the more knowledge you will acquire. This is especially significant for learning as much as you can about underlying securities for example or to find as many details about the market that is constantly changing. Significance of the right source of information eventually becomes the key to your progress, even more, if the world of options trading is still new to you. We can say that there are two types of relevant resources for options trading. The first one includes traditional resources such as magazines, newsletters, and newspapers. The second type is newer, it has a variety of options and these kinds of resources are mostly referred to as online resources.

The Internet offers a variety of free content, which is why many investors see it as their first stop whenever they need some kind of information. Further technology development also had a huge impact on the amount of information, tools, and possibilities that a person can access so using apps for education and trading, in general, has become a common thing. In the following text, we will list some of the most relevant option trading resources divided into the categories we explained above.

Even though they are considered to be more traditional, magazines, newspapers, newsletters, are still popular for research, for both experienced investors and beginners on the market. It is useful to know that many newsletters offer paid services such as recommendations, picks, research of certain categories, and other relevant information.

We will start with the magazines. Some of them such as Forbes are still one of the greatest and strongest magazines in the world for this matter. So, we have Fortune, Forbes, Consumer Money Adviser, Bloomberg BusinessWeek, Kiplinger's, and Fast Company as some of the most relevant magazines today. Newspapers that you might find useful are the Financial Times, the Wall Street Journal, The Washington Post, Value Line, and Barron's.

Some of the most recommended ones are ETF Trader, Market Watch Options Trader, The Proactive Fund Investor, Hulbert Interactive, The Technical Indicator, The Prudent Speculator, Dow Theory Forecasts, and Global Resources Trading

When it comes to online resources, they are probably the most frequent source of information for everything, not only for options trading. However, it is possible to find numerous websites that offer research that is up to date. Many of these analyses and other useful data can be found for free.

Technology development made many things easier with trading. Many apps have emerged and enabled investors to keep a close track of their investments at all times. It is important to know that there are apps that are not only for investment but for brokerage companies too. In the following text, you can find some of the investment apps that are most frequently used and that have excellent feedback.

How to avoid costly mistakes

Losing profit is not something that you want as an investor since the main purpose of options trading is to make money not the other way around. To do so, some tips can help you avoid mistakes that can be costly.

First of all, don't invest more capital than you are ready to lose. Keep in mind that trading options don't go without risks. There aren't any guarantees that the propositions that you'll face will gain you anything and your decisions are based on the hunch. Furthermore, if you don't have good timing and your hunch isn't right, you can lose the entire investment, not only the cash you were expecting to earn. The best way to avoid this kind of scenario is to start small. It is recommended that you use no more than 15 percent of your total portfolio on options trading.

The second tip that you should be aware of at all times is that good research gets the job done. If somebody says that it is a good idea to invest in options and you rush in and make an order without thinking it through, once more, you can lose more than you could earn. You should make your research and decide based on facts before you start trading.

There is another thing that you should be mindful of. No matter the strategy you choose for options trading, you should always try to adjust it to the current condition on the market. Not all strategies work in all environments which is why you must be up to date with circumstances in the world of finance and you have to adapt accordingly.

Without a proper exit strategy, it is useless to talk about successful business in options trading. You need to make a plan that you will follow through regardless of your emotions. Rational decisions are the main factor in trade, being emotional and making fast decisions out of rage or spite or feeling of insecurity can only make things worse. Stick to the plan you figured before you started trading because it should have both downside and upside points along with the timeframe for its execution. Just like you shouldn't let negative feelings influence your decision-making, you shouldn't allow the feeling of over-confidence in gaining large profits to pull you back from the path you have set for yourself. When it comes to risks, there is no need to take more risks than necessary, which means that the level of risk should be as big as your comfort with it. The level of risk tolerance is different for everyone; it is an individual think and only the investor himself can set its limit. Try to estimate that level and then choose all further actions accordingly. It is the safest premise to base your decisions on without being too insecure about every choice you make.

Chapter 8

Analyzing Mood Swing in the Market

The market is a chaotic place with many traders vying for dominance over one another. There are countless strategies and time frames in play and at any point, it is close to impossible to determine who will emerge with the upper hand. In such an environment, how is it then possible to make any money? After all, if everything is unpredictable, how can you get your picks right?

Well, this is where thinking in terms of probabilities comes into play. While you cannot get every single bet right, as long as you get enough right and make enough money on those to offset your losses, you will make money in the long run.

It's not about getting one or two right. It's about executing the strategy with the best odds of winning over and over again and ensuring that your math works out with regards to the relationship between your win rate and average win.

So, it comes down to finding patterns that repeat themselves over time in the markets. What causes these patterns? Well, the other traders of course! To put it more accurately, the orders that the other traders place in the market are what create patterns that repeat themselves over time.

The first step to understanding these patterns is to understand what trends and ranges are. Identifying them and learning to spot when they transition into one another will give you a massive leg up not only with your options trading but also with directional trading.

Trends

In theory spotting, a trend is simple enough. Look left to right and if the price is headed up or down, it's a trend. Well, sometimes it is that simple. However, for the majority of the time you have both with and counter-trend forces operating in the market. It is possible to have long counter-trend reactions within a larger trend and sometimes, depending on the time frame you're in, these counter-trend reactions take up the majority of your screen space.

Trend vs. Range

This is a chart of the UK100 CFD, which mimics the FTSE 100, on the four-hour time frame. Three-quarters of the chart is a downtrend and the last quarter is a wild uptrend. Using the looking left to the right guideline, we'd conclude that this instrument is in a range. Is that true though?

Just looking at that chart, you can see that short-term momentum is bullish. So, if you were considering taking a trade on this, would you implement a range strategy or a trending one? This is exactly the sort of thing that catches traders up.

The key to deciphering trends is to watch for two things: counter-trend participation quality and turning points. Let's tackle counter-trend participation first.

Counter Trend Participation

When a new trend begins, the market experiences an extremely imbalanced order flow that is tilted towards one side. There's isn't much counter-trend participation against this seeming tidal wave of with trend orders. Price marches on without any opposition and experiences only a few hiccups.

As time goes on though, the trend forces run out of steam and have to take breaks to gather themselves. This is where counter-trend traders start testing the trend and trying to see how far back into the trend they can go. While it is unrealistic to expect a full reversal at this point, the quality of the correction or pushback tells us a lot about the strength distribution between the with and counter-trend forces.

Eventually, the counter-trend players manage to push so far back against the trend that a stalemate results in the market. The counter-trend forces are equally balanced and thus the trend comes to an end. After all, you need an imbalance for the market to tip one way or another and a balanced order flow is only going to result in a sideways market.

While all this is going on behind the scenes, the price chart is what records the push and pull between these two forces. Using the price chart, we can not only anticipate when a trend is coming to an end but also how long it could potentially take before it does. This second factor, which helps us estimate the time it could take, is invaluable from an options perspective, especially if you're using a horizontal spread strategy.

In all cases, the greater the number of them, the greater the counter-trend participation in the market. The closer a trend is to end, the greater the counter-trend participation. Thus, the minute you begin to see price move into a large, sideways move with an equal number of buyers and sellers in it, you can be sure that some form of redistribution is going on.

Mind you, the trend might continue or reverse. Either way, it doesn't matter. What matters is that you know the trend is weak and that now is probably not the time to be banking on-trend strategies.

Starting from the left, we can see that there are close to no counter-trend bars, bearish in this case, and the bulls make easy progress. Note the angle with which the bulls proceed upwards.

Then comes the first major correction and the counter-trend players push back against the last third of the bull move. Notice how strong the bearish bars are and note their character compared to the bullish bars.

The bulls recover and push the price higher at the original angle and without any bearish presence, which seems odd. This is soon explained as the bears' slam price back down and for a while, it looks as if they've managed to form a V top reversal in the trend, which is an extremely rare occurrence.

The price action that follows is a more accurate reflection of the power in the market, with both bulls and bears sharing chunks of the order flow, with overall order flow in the bull's favor but only just. Price here is certainly in an uptrend but looking at the extent of the bearish pushbacks, perhaps we should be on our guard for a bearish reversal. After all order flow is looking pretty sideways at this point.

So how would we approach an options strategy with the chart in the state it is in at the extreme right? Well, for one, any strategy that requires an option beyond the near month is out of the question, given the probability of it turning. Secondly, looking at the order flow, it does seem to be following a channel, doesn't it?

While the channel isn't very clean, if you were aggressive enough, you could consider deploying a collar with the strike prices above and below this channel to take advantage of the price movement. You could also employ some moderately bullish strategies as price approaches the bottom of this channel and figuring out the extent of the bull move is easier thanks to you being able to reference the top of the channel.

As the price moves in this channel, it's all well and good. Eventually, though, we know that the trend has to flip. How do we know when this happens?

Turning Points

As bulls and bears struggle over who gets to control the order flow, price swings up and down. You will notice that every time price comes back into the 6427-6349 zone, the bulls seem to step in masse and repulse the bears.

This tells us that the bulls are willing to defend this level in large numbers and strongly at that. Given the number of times the bears have tested this level, we can safely assume that above this level, bullish strength is a bit weak. However, at this level, it is as if the bulls have retreated and are treating this as a sort of last resort, for the trend to be maintained. You can see where I'm going with this.

If this level were to be breached by the bears, it is a good bet that a large number of bulls will be taken out. In martial terms, the largest army of bulls has been marshaled at this level. If this force is defeated, it is unlikely that there's going to be too much resistance to the bears below this level.

This zone, in short, is a turning point. If price breaches this zone decisively, we can safely assume that the bears have moved in and control the majority of the order flow.

Turning Point Breached

The decisive turning point zone is marked by the two horizontal lines and the price touches this level twice more and is repulsed by the bulls. Notice how the last bounce before the level breaks produces an extremely weak bullish bounce and price simply caves through this. Notice the strength with which the bear breakthrough.

The FTSE was in a longer uptrend on the weekly chart, so the bulls aren't completely done yet. However, as far as the daily the timeframe is concerned, notice how price retests that same level but this time around, it acts as resistance instead of support.

For now, we can conclude that as long as the price remains below the turning point, we are bearishly biased. You can see this by looking at the angle with which bulls push back as well as, the lack of strong bearish participation on the push upwards.

This doesn't mean we go ahead and pencil in a bull move and start implementing strategies that take advantage of the upcoming bullish move. Remember, nothing is for certain in the markets. Don't change your bias or strategy until the turning point decisively breaks.

Some key things to note here are that a turning point is always a major S/R level. It is usually a swing point where a large number of trend forces gather to support the trend. This will not always be the case, so don't make the mistake of hanging on to older turning points.

The current order flow and price action are what matters the most, so pay attention to that above all else. Also, note how the candles that test this level all have wicks on top of them.

This indicates that the bears are quite strong here and that any subsequent attack will be handled the same way until the level breaks. Do we know when the level will break? Well, we can't say with any accuracy. However, we can estimate the probability of it breaking.

The latest upswing has seen very little bearish pushback, comparatively speaking, and the push into the level is strong.

Instinct would say that there's one more rejection left here. However, who knows? Until the level breaks, we stay bearish. When the level breaks, we switch to the bullish side.

Putting it all Together

So now we're ready to put all of this together into one coherent package. Your analysis should always begin with determining the current state of the market. Ranges are pretty straightforward to spot, and they occur either within big pullbacks in trends or at the end of trends.

Chapter 9

Options Trading Strategies

Options Strategies

We are now going to leave the world of selling options and go back to the one that most people are interested in, which is the world of trading options. We are going to have a look at strategies that can be used to increase the odds of profits when trading options. In reality, some of these strategies involve buying and selling options at the same time. Keep in mind that these techniques will require a higher-level designation from your broker. So, it might not be something you can use right away if you are a beginner.

Strangles

One of the simplest strategies that go beyond simply buying options, hoping to profit on moves of the underlying share price, is called a strangle. This strategy involves buying a call option and a put option simultaneously. They will have the same expiration dates, but different strike prices. If the price of the stock rises the put option will expire worthless (but of course it may still hold a small amount of value when you closed your position, and you can sell it and recoup some of the loss). But you will make a profit off the call option. On the other hand, if the stock price declines, the call option will expire worthlessly, but you can make a profit from the put option.

In this case, you can make substantial profits no matter which way the stock moves, but the larger the move, the more profits. On the upside, the profit potential is theoretically unlimited. On the downside, the stock could theoretically fall to zero, so there is a limit, but potential gains are substantial. The breakeven price on the upside is the strike price of the call plus the amount of the two premiums settled for the options. If the stock price declines the breakeven price would be the difference between the strike value of the put option and the sum of the two premiums paid for the options.

Straddles

When you purchase a call and a put option with similar strike amounts and expiration dates, this is called a straddle. The idea here is that the trader is hoping the share price will either rise or fall by a significant amount. It won't matter which way the price moves. Again, if the price rises the put option will expire worthless, if the price falls the call option will expire worthlessly. For example, suppose a stock is trading at $100 a share. We can buy at the money call and put options that expire in 30 days. The price of the call and put options would be $344 and $342 respectively, for a total investment of $686. With 20 days left to expiration, suppose the share price rises to $107. Then the call is priced at $766, and the put is at $65. We can sell them both at this time, for $831, and make a profit of $145.

Suppose that, instead of at 20 days to expiration, the share price dropped to $92. In that case, the call is priced at $39, and the put is priced at $837. We can sell them for $876, making a profit of $190.

So, although the profits are modest compared to a situation where we had speculated correctly on the directional move of the stock and bought only calls or puts, this way we profit no matter which way the share price moves. The downside to this strategy is that the share price may not move in a big enough way to make profits possible. Remember that extrinsic value will be declining for both the call and the put options.

Selling covered calls against LEAPS and other LEAPS Strategies

A LEAP is a long-term option that is option that expires at a date that is two years in the future. They are regular options otherwise, but you can do some interesting things with LEAPS. Because the expiration date is so far away, they cost a lot more. Looking at Apple, call options with a $195 strike price that expires in two years are selling for $28.28 (for a total price of $2,828). While that seems expensive, consider that 100 shares of Apple would cost $19,422 at the time of writing.

If you buy in the money LEAPS, then you can use them to sell covered calls. This is an interesting strategy that lets you earn premium income without having bought the shares of stock.

LEAPS can also be used for other investing strategies. For example, if Apple is trading at $194, we can buy a LEAP option for $3,479 with a strike price of $190 that expires in two

years. If, at some point during those two years, the share price rose to $200 we could exercise the option and buy the shares at $190, saving $10 a share. Also, at the same time, we could have been selling covered calls against the LEAPS.

Buying Put Options as Insurance

A put option gives you the right to sell shares of stock at a certain price. Suppose that you wanted to ensure your investment in Apple stock, and you had purchased 100 shares at $191 a share, for a total investment of $19,000. You are worried that the share price is going to drop and so you could buy a put option as a kind of insurance. Looking ahead, you see a put option with a $190 strike price for $4.10. So, you spend $410 and buy the put option.

Should the price of Apple shares suddenly tumble you could exercise your right under the put option to dispose of your shares by selling at the strike price to minimize your losses.

Suppose you wake up one morning and the share price has dropped to $170 for some reason. Had you not bought the option you could have tried to get rid of your shares now and take a loss of $21 a share. But, since you bought the put option, you can sell your shares for $190 a share. That is a $1 loss since you purchased the shares at $191. However, you also have to consider the premium paid for the put options contract, which was $4.10. So, your total loss would be $5.10 a share, but that is still less than the loss of $21 a share that you would have suffered selling the shares on the market at the $170 price. When investors buy stock and a put at the same time, it is called a married put.

Spreads

Spreads involve buying and selling options simultaneously. This is a more complicated options strategy that is only used by advanced traders. You will have to get a high-level designation with your brokerage to use this type of strategy. We won't go into details because these methods are beyond the scope of junior options traders, but we will briefly mention some of the more popular methods so that you can have some awareness.

One of the interesting things about spreads is they can be used by level 3 traders to earn a regular income from options. If you think the price of a stock is going to stay the same or rise, you sell a put credit spread. You sell a higher-priced option and buy a lower-priced option at the same time. The difference in option prices is your profit. There is a chance of loss if the price drops to the strike price of the puts (and you could get assigned if it goes below the strike price of the put option you sold). You can buy back the spread, in that case, to avoid getting assigned.

If you think that the price of a stock is going to drop you can sell to open a credit spread. In this case, you are hoping the price of the stock is going to stay the same or drop. You sell a call with a low strike price and buy a call with a high strike price (both out of the money). The price difference is your profit, and losses are capped.

We can also consider more complicated spreads.

For example, you can use a diagonal spread with calls. This means you buy a call that has a shorter expiration date but a higher strike amount, and then you sell a call with a longer expiration date and a lower strike price. This is done in such a way that you earn more, from selling the call, than you spend on buying the call for a considerable strike amount, and so you get a net credit to your account.

Spreads can become quite complicated, and there are many different types of spreads. If a trader thinks that the price of a stock will only go up a small amount, they can do a bull call spread. Profit and loss are capped in this case. The two options would have the same expiration date.

If you sell a call with a lower strike price and simultaneously buy a call with a high strike price, this is called a bear call spread. You seek to profit if the underlying stock drops in price. This can also be done by using two put options. In that case, you buy a put option that has a higher strike and sell a put option with a lower strike price.

A bull spread involves attempting to profit when the price of the stock rises by a small amount. In this case, you can also use either two call options or two put options. You buy an option with a lower strike price while selling an option with a higher strike price.

Spreads can be combined in more complicated ways. An iron

butterfly combines a bear call spread with a bear puts spread. The purpose of doing this is to generate steady income while minimizing the risk of loss.

An iron condor uses a put spread, and a call spread together. There would be four options simultaneously, with the same expiration dates but different strike prices. It involves selling both sides (calls and puts).

Chapter 10

FAQ

Here is a collection of questions. I hope this will save you time and answer most of the questions that may arise in your mind after you are done with the book.

Q: What time-frame do I use for my charts?

A: I use a 3 month-daily time frame for all my charts. This works perfectly with the expiration cycles I choose for my trades (i.e. between 30 - 60 days)

Q: How do I decide what strike prices to use for my debit spreads?

A: I try to buy 1 strike in the money and sell 1 strikeout of the money to complete my debit spread. If that is not possible, I may take the liberty of buying 1 strike ATM and 1 strike OTM too. I try not to be too obsessive about the strikes as the entry point is selected by technical analysis.

Q: Do I take 100% profit for my trades? Or do I sometimes close them early for a smaller profit?

A: When the trade immediately starts going in my direction after I put it on, and my spread is deep-in-the-money as expiration nears, I take 100% profits.

On the other hand, sometimes the position bounces back and forth between profits and losses. One day it may show a profit, and a few days later it may show a loss. In these situations where the market direction is not very clear and the trade keeps me guessing if I did it right or not, I may exit as soon as I hit 50% - 70% of the max possible profit.

Q: How do I scale my system? As my account size grows bigger, do I trade more contracts to take higher risks (and reap bigger rewards)?

A: You will notice that when I start with $2500, my trades typically have 1 contract and yield $300-$400. The risk I am taking with these trades also falls in the same range.

As my account size grows bigger (around $10,000), my trade sizes/risk/reward also gets bigger. To accomplish this, I don't trade more contracts. I simply increase the width of my spreads. e.g. When my net liq is around $2500, I might buy a $500 - $510 Call Debit spread on XYZ stock. In this case, I might be risking $250 to make $250. But as my account size grows bigger, the same spread might look like a $500 - $520 Call Debit spread, where I will be risking $1000 to make $1000. In my experience, widening the spread as opposed to increasing the number of contracts yields better results and allows you to close your profitable positions much faster.

Q: Can you use DITM (Deep-In-The-Money) Calls and Puts instead of Debit Spreads with this strategy?

A: Yes, you can use DITM options with my trading signals. However, I would encourage you to use a paper-trading account and compare how DITM options perform as opposed to debit spreads. In my opinion, spreads will yield way better and consistent results than simply buying calls or puts.

Q: Have I tried these methodologies on futures or indexes?

A: I don't trade futures, so have never tried these methodologies on the futures market. However, I don't see any reason why these methods will not work on any market.

As far as Indexes are concerned, yes, I actively trade many indexes like SPY, RUT, TLT, IYR, etc. and my methods yield great results with these. In fact, during earnings season when I don't trade stocks, I switch exclusively to indexes.

Q: Do I invest on behalf of others on a profit-sharing basis?

A: Unfortunately, I don't do this. My goal is to share my experiences and methodology with you and enable you to achieve similar results by improving your skillset. I do provide constant email support and guidance to our paid members throughout my challenges.

Q: Will there be a monthly fee to participate in the upcoming $25K options challenges?

A: Although, I have made the 2019 challenge available for free as I near the finish line, you will have an opportunity to follow my live trades for future Options Challenges. The pricing is currently being worked on.

Conclusion

Many years ago, people working for house banking, financial institutions, and brokerages did only regular trading in the stock market. Brokers also simplified matters for the average investor willing to go into trading with the advent of the internet and the rise of online trading houses.

Day trading can be very lucrative if you know how to do it properly, and in the Australian market, it is trendy. Day trading is the buying and selling of an asset during one business day. This method of trading allows you to close all positions at the end of each working day and then continue throughout the day following. Trading on a day is not confined to a single market but is common in stock markets and forex. Day traders buy and sell several commodities in a single day, or even multiple times a day. They use these strategies to take advantage of any price changes in currencies or liquid stocks, no matter how low. You have to be a fast decision-maker as a day trader, and be able to conduct multiple trades every time for a small profit.

Day trading isn't a sport, and can't be. You have to be careful about it and stick to it. Because you need to keep monitoring the open opportunities business trend, you need to have plenty of time during the day to devote to this company.

Be mindful of the market you are on. Try to focus on a few chosen business or financial instruments and focus on them. Over time, you'll be tuned to the market or resources you've decided to focus on. You are going to develop a sixth sense of your market conditions.

The trick is to plan. Always train yourself properly before trading the next day. You still need to do the groundwork necessary; for instance, giving yourself a briefing on how, where, and when you will conduct your trade policy. Having an idea where to put the loss of your stop would make sure you cover your loss point for the day. So you can spend the bulk of the day doing business for profit.

Make sure you stick to your business plan. This will require enormous discipline on your part but is an important part of a successful day trader. There's no easy way to control your greed. This needs a high degree of self-control. Don't try to optimize every single trading point. It is also easier to let go. A winning trade in a fast-changing market can quickly turn into a loss. Often you have to cut a losing role and shouldn't hesitate when the time comes. Taking some small losses is better than waiting for a significant loss to strike you and wipe out your entire wealth.

It's also crucial you never try to capture the market at all. If you miss a good trade for some reason, because you've been late, don't jump in at the latter point. You may be doing it at the high end or low end of the deal by the time you reach the market. Miss the exchange and go back to work the next day. Never engage in a transaction unless you are sure about what you are doing. Do not trade for the merchant's sake or that you are searching for excitement.

To put it another way, do not overtrade. Never trade in trend at the top or bottom end. The market is often dynamic and can go higher or lower than expected. If you're straying from the trend spectrum, you might be on the wrong side of the curve.

Protecting your wealth will still be your priority number one. Rentability is secondary to that. Controlling your losses will help ensure you have another day to live to trade. If you keep chasing profits and the market backtracks unexpectedly, you may find that there would be a high proportion of your resources at risk.

Take note of news reports coming up. In particular, keeping an open position before releasing any news, which may influence the market is a bad idea. If you can second-guess the economy, you can never know until the news is released what direction the economy can head in.

CPSIA information can be obtained
at www.ICGtesting.com
Printed in the USA
LVHW050710090421
683977LV00015B/552